TESSA KR.

THE BATTLE OF WATERLOO ROAD

Illustrated by
Adrienne Geoghegan

OXFORD
UNIVERSITY PRESS

OXFORD
UNIVERSITY PRESS

Great Clarendon Street, Oxford OX2 6DP

Oxford University Press is a department of the University of Oxford.
It furthers the University's objective of excellence in research, scholarship,
and education by publishing worldwide in

Oxford New York

Athens Auckland Bangkok Bogotá Buenos Aires Calcutta
Cape Town Chennai Dar es Salaam Delhi Florence Hong Kong Istanbul
Karachi Kuala Lumpur Madrid Melbourne Mexico City Mumbai
Nairobi Paris São Paulo Shanghai Singapore Taipei Tokyo Toronto Warsaw

and associated companies in Berlin Ibadan

Oxford is a trade mark of Oxford University Press
in the UK and in certain other countries

British Library Cataloguing in Publication Data
Data available

ISBN 0 19 915952 1

Printed in Hong Kong

Available in packs

Year 4 / Primary 5 Pack of Six (one of each book) ISBN 0 19 915955 6
Year 4 / Primary 5 Class Pack (six of each book)   ISBN 0 19 915956 4

Contents

1
Football Mad

Tod thought history was one big yawn.

It was so bo-o-o-ring, having to sit here in this stuffy classroom when he could be outside playing football. But no, he had to sit and listen to Mrs Batsford – otherwise known as Old Batty – going on and on about stupid history. He opened his mouth in a long, silent yawn. Aaaaaaaaah!

"Tod Winters!" Old Batty's voice

boomed across the room. "Am I
sending you to sleep?"

He jerked upright. "Er – no, Mrs
Batsford. Sorry, Mrs Batsford."

The rest of the class giggled.

"I certainly hope not," she snapped.
"Because I want you to write down as
much as you know about Napoleon."

Tod looked blank. "Napoleon?"

Mrs Batsford sighed. "I've been
talking about Napoleon for the past
twenty minutes. He was a great general
who also became the Emperor of
France. If you look on the wall you can
see a picture of him."

Tod looked on the wall. The man in
the picture wore tight white trousers
and a black hat shaped like an upturned
boat. His right hand was tucked into his
waistcoat.

Mrs Batsford rose from her desk.

"Here are some words to help you."

First she wrote FRANCE and EMPEROR on the board. Then, on another line, BATTLE and WATERLOO. She also drew a picture.

Waterloo?

Wasn't that the name of the school they were playing football against next Saturday? Waterloo Road v St Joseph's, Tod's team. Tod grinned to himself. That was going to be a battle all right!

Mr Jenks, their soccer coach, had warned them that Waterloo Road was one of the strongest teams around.

Tod closed his eyes. Inside his head he could see it happening, just as if he was watching it on TV. If Waterloo Road won the toss, he would intercept at once and get the ball away from them. Next he would run fast with it down the left wing... and then what? Tod frowned. St Joseph's team needed some kind of –

"Strategy," said Mrs Batsford.

Tod opened his eyes and blinked. Old Batty couldn't possibly have said "strategy". He must have imagined it. But no, she'd actually written it up on the board: STRATEGY.

She gave him a hard look. "Tod, do you know what 'strategy' means?"

"Yes, Mrs Batsford."

Of course he knew! "Strategy" meant having a plan of action. Working out the moves in advance in order to defeat the opposing side. At least, that's what it meant in football.

But what did strategy have to do with Napoleon?

"Time and again," she went on, "Napoleon defeated the enemy by having a brilliant strategy."

Oh, so that was it. Same thing really. A plan of action...

In his mind he was back on the football pitch. He could almost feel the ball bounce off his foot as he walloped it into the net...

"Time to stop," said Mrs Batsford. "Clare, will you collect the books, please?"

Tod came back to earth with a jolt.

Clare James stopped beside him. She

stared down at his exercise book.
"Please, Mrs Batsford," she said. "Tod
hasn't written anything."

"Nothing at all?"

"Well, he's written down 'Waterloo'
and 'strategy'. And he's done a drawing
of a football."

Mrs Batsford sighed. "Tod, you're
football mad. Do you never think
about anything else? There are more
important things in life, you know."

Tod kept quiet, but he knew she was wrong. There wasn't anything more important in life than football. At least, not in *his* life. This was his first season as captain of St Joseph's Junior XI and he meant to be their most successful captain ever.

Mrs Batsford went on, "I want you to stay in during break and write at least half a page on the subject of Napoleon. The others may go."

"Bad luck, mate," muttered Jimbo as he passed Tod's desk.

Jimbo was his best friend and St Joseph's goalkeeper.

When everyone else had left, Tod stared down at the blank page. What could he write? He didn't know anything about Napoleon, except that he was a famous French general. And an emperor. And good at strategy ...

"Brilliant," said a voice. "Not just good. Brilliant. You heard what your teacher said."

Tod looked up. He'd thought he was alone in the room. But no, there was a man sitting on the edge of Mrs Batsford's desk, swinging one leg. A man wearing tight white trousers and a dark hat shaped like an upturned boat. A man with his right hand tucked into his waistcoat.

Napoleon!

2
Mon Ami

Tod stared at him. "Are you a ghost?"

Napoleon removed his hat for a moment and smoothed his hair forward over his forehead. "Do I look like a ghost? Can you see through me? Am I clanking chains or making a wailing noise?"

"Well, no. But – "

"Then I can't be a ghost, can I?" Napoleon slid off Mrs Batsford's desk

and came to look over Tod's shoulder.
"You don't seem to have
written much."

"I can't think of
anything to say."

"*Mon ami*, I've had whole books
written about me! I was the Emperor
of France and the greatest general who
ever lived. Surely you can think of
something?"

Tod felt embarrassed. "Sorry, but
I'm no good at history. It's too – well,
boring. I prefer football."

"So I see." Napoleon pointed a short, stubby finger at Tod's drawing. "But you're also interested in strategy, it seems. I can teach you a lot about strategy. First you must get to know your enemy. Find out what their weaknesses are."

He went back to Mrs Batsford's desk. "Tell me, *mon ami*, who is your enemy?"

"Waterloo Road Juniors," said Tod.

"Ugh!" Napoleon shuddered. "Just about the only battle I ever lost and they name a school after it! So, what do you know about them?"

"Not much. This is the first match of the season."

"Then you must find out. Send a spy into their camp." Napoleon dusted off his hat again and put it back on his head. "Meantime you'd better get on with your work, *mon ami*."

"You keep calling me that," Tod said. "But I don't know what it means. Is it French or something?"

"Of course it's French!" Napoleon looked shocked. "*Mon ami* means 'my friend'. Now, you'd better write something quickly before your teacher comes back."

"But I still don't know what to say."

Napoleon sighed. "I will tell you. Start writing."

At the end of break the other kids came bursting back into the room. "You'll never guess what's happened," said Jimbo, sitting down at the next table. "Mr Jenks has broken his leg."

"He fell off a ladder," said George Hardcastle. "And there's no chance they'll let him out of hospital before the match on Saturday. Tod, what are we going to do without a coach?"

Tod put down his pen. It was bad news about Mr Jenks, of course it was, but at the moment his mind was full of something else. "Jimbo, look!" he whispered.

"Where?" asked Jimbo.

"Old Batty's desk. Look who's sitting there."

"Oh, glory!" Jimbo hastily bent his head over his book. "I never saw her come in."

"Saw her ...?" Tod looked up.

Napoleon had vanished. In his place sat Mrs Batsford, drumming her fingers on the desk. "Quiet, please. Tod, bring me your history book."

Tod gave her his book, his mind buzzing with questions. Where was Napoleon? Was he hiding somewhere? Or had he really been a ghost after all?

Mrs Batsford stared down at what he had written. "Two whole pages! Tod, you clearly knew more about Napoleon than I thought. Indeed, you seem to know certain facts I never even mentioned." She gave him a suspicious look. "Did you copy this out of a book?"

"No, Mrs Batsford."

She frowned. "It's not like you to cheat. Go back to your place. We'll talk about this later, when I've had time to think about it."

Her words hung like a cloud over Tod for the rest of the afternoon. She thought he had cheated – and all because he knew more about Napoleon than she did. But how could he possibly explain?

After school, when Tod joined Jimbo and George for a football practice, he thought of telling them about Napoleon but decided against it. They'd think he'd gone mad. In any case they only had one thing on their minds – Saturday's match.

"We don't stand a chance," George said gloomily. "Not now we've lost our coach."

"We don't need a coach," said Tod. "Mr Jenks wasn't all that good anyway.

I'm the captain, I'll tell you what to do."

"Like what?" asked Jimbo.

"Well ... first we've got to get to know the enemy."

"Enemy?"

"Waterloo Road Juniors. Find out what their weaknesses are."

George looked puzzled. "How can we do that, Tod?"

"Send a spy into their camp. George, don't you have a cousin at Waterloo Road?"

"Yeah, she's called Alice."

"A girl!" Jimbo groaned. "She'd be no use as a spy. What do girls know about football?"

"Quite a lot, if you mean Alice. She's mad about it."

"I think we should give it a chance," said Tod. "George, see if you can get her to tell you about the Waterloo Road team. Then we can work out our strategy."

3

A Faint Smell of Perfume

At teatime his older sister Lucy announced, "Tod was kept in at break today."

Tod glared at her. That was the worst of having a sister at the same school. He couldn't keep anything secret.

Mum looked at him inquiringly. "Why was that?"

"Old Batty made me stay behind and

write about Napoleon," Todd told her. With pride he added, "I wrote two pages."

"Two pages?" Lucy stared at him. "But you don't know enough to write two pages about anything. Except football, of course."

"I told you, this was about Napoleon," said Tod. "I know a lot about Napoleon."

"Do you?" Mum looked surprised. "And was Old Batty – er, Mrs Batsford – pleased?"

"Mmm," mumbled Tod.

Luckily Lucy started talking about Mr Jenks, who was her class teacher, breaking his leg. But Tod couldn't help remembering what Mrs Batsford had said. *We'll talk about this later, when I've had time to think about it.* What did she mean by "later"? Tomorrow?

That night he lay awake for a long time, staring round his room. Football posters lined the walls, together with pictures of his favourite players. Yet for once Tod wasn't thinking about football. He was thinking about Napoleon. Could it have been a dream? Perhaps, when he was left alone in the classroom, he had fallen asleep?

But he couldn't have dreamed writing those two pages, because Old Batty had actually read them. Nor could he have made up French words he'd never heard before. Words like…

"Mon ami."

At first he thought he must have spoken aloud. But then he saw Napoleon sitting on the end of his bed. Tod stared at him, dumbstruck. The Emperor looked far too solid to be a dream. The end of the bed had sunk under his weight and there was a faint smell of perfume in the room. A perfume his grandmother sometimes used ...

Eau de Cologne!

Napoleon went on, "Tell me, *mon ami*, did your teacher like that piece we wrote?"

"Not really," said Tod when he had recovered from his shock. "She believes I copied it out of a book. She's going to talk to me later when she's had time to think about it."

"Ah!" said Napoleon. "That means she's going to check every book in the classroom to see where you got your information. But of course she won't find anything."

"Won't she?"

He shook his head. "What I told you to write – that story about my childhood in Corsica – she won't find

in any book. So that will prove you didn't copy it. She'll have to apologize."

Tod began to feel better. "You really think so?"

"I'm certain of it." Napoleon took a small box out of his pocket and opened the lid. From inside he took what looked like an old black bootlace and popped it into his mouth.

"Mmm, delicious! Want some?" He held out the box to Tod.

"What is it?"

"Liquorice. Wonderful for calming the nerves. Go on, try it."

Tod took a piece and put it into his mouth.

"Now about this football match against Waterloo Road ..." Napoleon shuddered. "Oh, how I hate that name! It makes me feel sick every time I hear it. You have to win this battle, *mon ami*, for my sake."

"I'll do my best," said Tod. "But Mr Jenks says they're one of the strongest teams around."

"Don't let that worry you," said Napoleon. "I often fought battles against armies that were stronger than mine. I defeated them by moving fast and striking where they least expected, on their weakest flank."

Tod nodded. "That's what I plan to do. Our strategy – "

"Tod?" The door opened and Mum's head appeared.

"Oh, I thought I heard you talking to someone. But you're alone."

Tod gulped so hard he choked on the piece of liquorice.

"Be careful. Talking to yourself is the first sign of madness, so they say." Mum laughed and switched off the light. "Sweet dreams."

Tod leaned back in the darkness. What Mum had said was true, he was alone in the room. There was no one sitting on the end of his bed. Napoleon had vanished the instant Mum opened the door. All he had left behind was a faint smell of *eau de Cologne*.

4

Exercises

"I spoke to Alice," George said on the way into school next morning. "She says the Waterloo Road team is the best."

"What about their weaknesses?" asked Tod.

"She says they don't have any."

Jimbo groaned. "Didn't you find out anything useful?"

George thought hard. He said, "Their

strip is green and yellow. Oh, and their captain's name is Jo Marshall."

Tod frowned. "I don't think I know him."

"It's not a him, it's a her. Jo's short for Josephine."

"A girl?" Jimbo looked shocked. "But – but *we* don't have any girls in our team. Mr Jenks wouldn't allow it."

"Alice says Mr Jenks is out-of-date. Their coach is a woman too." George added defiantly, "Her name's Miss Cannon."

Tod was speechless. He felt sure Napoleon had never had to fight against women at the Battle of Waterloo. Somehow this made everything different.

When they reached the classroom George said, "I just remembered. They have a team practice after school every

Wednesday. We could go and spy on them if you want."

"Today's Wednesday," said Jimbo. "I can go. How about you, Tod?"

He just had time to say, "Yeah, right," before Mrs Batsford entered the room.

At break she asked him to stay behind. Perhaps she wants to apologize, he thought, remembering what Napoleon had said.

She waited until the others had left. "Now I want you to tell me the truth," she began. "That piece you wrote yesterday – you made most of it up, didn't you?"

"No, Mrs Batsford."

"Please don't lie to me, Tod. I've read a great many books about Napoleon and none of them said he stole peaches when he was a boy. So how could you possibly know that?"

Tod said nothing. She wouldn't believe him if he told her.

"Just as I thought," she said. "You made it up."

"No, I didn't," Tod protested. "I know a lot about Napoleon. Some things I didn't even write down."

Mrs Batsford sighed. "Such as?"

"Such as … he used to smell of *eau de Cologne.*"

"*Eau de Cologne?*"

"And liquorice. He ate a lot of liquorice. He said it calmed his nerves."

Mrs Batsford stared at him. "I do remember reading something …"

"And in battle," Tod went on quickly, "he liked to move fast and strike where least expected."

"Quite right. He did." She frowned. "I think I'd better keep your history book a little longer, Tod. If it turns out that I'm wrong I shall apologize. Now go and join the others."

Tod went before she had time to change her mind. So Napoleon had been right after all!

Tod, Jimbo and George propped their bikes against the wall. "There they are." George pointed to some distant figures. "And that's their coach, Miss Cannon, in the red tracksuit."

Jimbo shaded his eyes. "Looks like they're doing exercises. Knee-bends, press-ups, that sort of thing."

"That's to get themselves fit," George explained. "At the start of every practice they do exercises for at least ten minutes. Alice told me."

Tod grinned. "Must make them tired before they even start!"

"She says it did at the beginning but not now. Look out, here they come!"

Hastily they ducked down behind the wall. The sound of running footsteps came closer.

The coach's voice called out,

"Stop! Right, now jogging on the spot."

After a while Tod slowly raised his head to take a look.

"Careful!" warned Jimbo. "They'll see you."

"No, they won't. They've got their backs to us."

They all peered over the wall. "There's my cousin Alice," said George. "And look, that must be Jo Marshall."

Tod had imagined Waterloo Road's captain as a big, tough girl with bony knees. To his surprise she was small and slim with long fair hair tied back in a ponytail.

"Right, team," shouted the coach. "Now run on ... "

But at that moment Alice turned round and saw the three boys watching over the wall. "Jo, look!" she called. "We're being spied on."

And the whole Waterloo Road team turned round to stare at them.

5

Short for Josephine

Jo Marshall's eyes opened wide, but she spoke in a friendly voice. "Hi. Do you want something?"

"Er – no, thanks," said Tod.

"Just looking," said Jimbo.

"We're going now," said George, backing away.

Alice pointed her finger at him. "That's my cousin. I told you he's been asking questions."

"You mean they're from St Joseph's?" Jo's voice grew sharper and less friendly. "So Alice was right. You *are* spying on us!"

Tod flushed. "Just happened to be cycling past," he muttered. "We saw you practising and thought we'd take a look, that's all."

"Oh, yes?" Clearly she didn't believe him. "Well, you've had your look so now you can push off."

"Yeah, push off!" growled the rest of the team.

"What's the matter?" called Miss Cannon. "I told you to keep running."

"Right, team. Let's go," said Jo with cool authority. But as they turned away she spoke directly to Tod. "See you Saturday." Somehow she made it sound like a threat.

"Yeah, Saturday." Tod tried to sound

equally threatening, but his voice came
out hoarse and uncertain. He climbed
on his bike and cycled off, followed by
Jimbo and George.

Jimbo said bitterly, "Fat lot of use
your cousin Alice turned out to be,
George."

"How could I know she was a double
agent?" George muttered, pedalling
furiously.

"Typical girl!" said Tod. But somehow

the words sounded hollow, perhaps because *these* girls were proving a lot less typical than he'd expected.

Shortly afterwards his front tyre went flat.

Tod stopped. Jimbo and George came back to see what had happened.

"Got a puncture," he told them. "Don't wait for me. No point in you being late as well."

They cycled off, eager to get home to their teas. Tod started to walk, pushing his bike.

"So? What did you find out?" Napoleon fell into step beside him.

Tod wasn't even surprised to see him. "Not much," he admitted. "They were just doing exercises. Running round the field. Getting fit."

"That means they'll be well prepared," said Napoleon. "A fit army

is always the hardest to conquer.
Anything else?"

"Their captain's a girl called Jo
Marshall. That's short for Josephine."

Napoleon stopped dead, staring at
him. "Did you say ... Josephine?"

"Yes. Why, what's wrong?"

"My first wife was called Josephine.
Lovely woman, but very strong-willed."
He frowned. "In my opinion it's a

mistake to allow women on to the battlefield."

"Trouble is, we still haven't really worked out our strategy," Tod admitted.

"In that case, *mon ami*, we'd better start now."

Napoleon put an arm around Tod's shoulders and they walked home together, still talking.

Mum and Lucy were in the kitchen when Tod arrived. "You're late," said Mum. "We've almost finished our tea."

"I got a flat tyre and had to walk home." Tod looked at her curiously. "Mum, did you ever want to play football when you were at school?"

She laughed. "No, I did not! I hated games – and I never had the slightest wish to play football."

"I do," Lucy said unexpectedly. "But Mr Jenks won't let me."

"In my opinion it's a mistake to allow women on to the battle – er, football field," said Tod. As Lucy lifted the milk jug as if to pour it over his head he added quickly, "I was only quoting Napoleon."

"Don't be daft," said Mum. "Napoleon never said that."

"Yes, he did. He said it – " Tod just managed to stop before he said "this afternoon". Instead he finished – "sometime. I saw it in a book."

Mum raised her eyebrows. "You really do seem to like Napoleon, don't you?"

"I thought you hated history," said Lucy.

"Oh, it's not so bad," said Tod with

a shrug. "Sometimes it can teach you quite useful things, like strategy."

Mum and Lucy exchanged a look as if to say, wonders will never cease!

6
Serious Training

Next morning at assembly Mrs Barker, the Headteacher, announced there would be a football practice after school for the Junior XI.

"As Mr Jenks is away it will be taken by your captain, Tod Winters," she said. "Well done, you boys, for organizing yourselves without a coach. I shall certainly come and cheer you on at Waterloo Road on Saturday."

Tod flushed with pride. He was determined to be the best coach the team had ever had, far better than old out-of-date Mr Jenks.

"Right, team," he said when they met in the playground after school. "Now for some serious training. We'll begin with jogging on the spot."

George said, "But that's what the Waterloo Road – "

"Shut up, George, and start jogging." Tod started himself, to set an example, and soon the others joined in. "We gotta get fit. A fit army is always the hardest to conquer."

"You make it sound like war," grumbled Jimbo.

"It *is* war!"

After jogging they did knee-bends and then press-ups. Jimbo said warningly, "Tod, we're being watched."

Tod looked round. "Who? Where?"

"Two girls. Over by the tree. I think one of them is George's cousin Alice."

"He's right," said George. "And the other's Jo Marshall. They've come to spy on us."

The whole team turned round to stare.

"Take no notice," said Tod. "Pretend they aren't there."

He told the team to gather round him so that the two girls could not overhear. "We've got to work on our strategy," he said in a low voice.

"Our what?" asked Mick Hodges, their centre forward.

"Our plan of action. I reckon we should move fast up the field on their right flank, then suddenly switch the attack to their left flank when they're least expecting it."

"What's he talking about?" asked Mick, frowning. "Right flank, left flank... I don't get it."

"Flank's another word for wing," Jimbo explained. "You know, like in a battle."

Tod went on. "Speed, that's our best weapon ..."

"They're getting nearer," said George. "Who are?"

"Those girls. I think they're trying to listen."

Tod swung round. George was right, Jo and Alice were now within hearing distance. He walked over to them.

"Are you spying on us?" he demanded.

"What if we are?" said Alice defiantly. "You spied on us yesterday, when you came to watch us practising."

"Leave it, Alice." Jo Marshall turned

to face Tod. "You're their captain, right?"

He nodded.

"It was bad luck, losing your coach. But it looks as if you're doing fine without him. Come on, Alice. Let's go." The two girls began to walk away.

"That told 'em!" Jimbo clapped Tod enthusiastically on the back. "You were great, captain!"

"Yeah, you were great!" The rest of the team gave a victory cheer – "We are the champions!" – loud enough to reach the ears of the departing girls.

But Tod didn't join in. Jo Marshall had seemed so cool and confident that he was suddenly filled with doubts about the match on Saturday. He tried to shake them off by shouting, "Right, now let's concentrate on our ball skills."

After the practice the rest of the team went home but Tod hung about for a while, quietly dribbling the ball around the playground.

Suddenly he noticed Napoleon leaning against the wall. "Were you watching?" he asked. "How did you think it went?"

"It went well, *mon ami*." Napoleon sighed heavily.

"You don't sound very sure."

Napoleon shook his head. "That name still worries me. Waterloo Road. I just hope history isn't going to repeat itself."

This made Tod feel even worse. Napoleon had lost the Battle of Waterloo, even he knew that. But he'd lost it against the Duke of Wellington, not against Josephine. Surely that made a difference?

7

The Last Battle

By Saturday Tod had begun to feel happier. His team was the best, he felt certain of it. And they were going to win, no doubt about it.

What's more, Mrs Batsford had told him yesterday that she'd checked out what he said about Napoleon and it was all perfectly correct. Napoleon had eaten liquorice to calm his nerves and every morning he splashed *eau de*

Cologne over himself. She apologized to Tod for doubting him and gave him top marks for the piece he'd written.

That afternoon he led his team on to the Waterloo Road pitch to the cheers of St Joseph's supporters. Among them he spotted Mum and Lucy, and nearby Mrs Barker, their Headteacher.

The referee, who was the Waterloo Road coach Miss Cannon, took a coin from her pocket. "Who's going to call?"

"He can," said Jo Marshall, nodding at Tod.

"Heads or tails?" The coin was already spinning.

"Heads," called Tod, and it was. Great! Even the toss had gone his way.

He took the kick-off himself and sent the ball over to George on the right wing. The plan was to pretend that the right wing was their strongest point of attack when in fact the real offensive would come from the left. But he hadn't reckoned on Jo Marshall's speed. Small and quick, she ran rings around poor George. Before he had a chance to stop her she had got the ball away from him and passed it down the pitch to one of their large, powerful-looking strikers. Soon afterwards, only five minutes into the game, came the first goal. *Waterloo Road 1, St Joseph's 0.*

Tod felt terrible. He urged his team to try harder. They must equalize as quickly as possible. But although St Joseph's managed to keep the game down their opponents' half of the pitch, somehow they failed to score. What had gone wrong? Their strategy didn't seem to be working.

Half-time came, not a moment too soon.

"It's not that bad," Tod told his gloomy-looking team. "We're only one goal down."

"Yeah, I'm sorry," said Jimbo. "But it came at me like a bullet. I couldn't stop it."

"'Course you couldn't. Nobody could. The important thing is to remember our strategy. Keep attacking on the left."

In the second half, to Tod's relief, Mick Hodges managed at last to break through their defences and score.

Waterloo Road 1, St Joseph's 1.

But soon afterwards, Waterloo Road scored another goal and Tod began to feel desperate. He thought he saw Napoleon on the touchline, cupping both hands round his mouth, but what was he shouting?

"*Change your strategy. Attack on the right!*"

Tod didn't stop to wonder whether he'd imagined it. After all, what had they got to lose?

"To me!" he yelled, and as soon as George passed him the ball he ran fast down the right wing, weaving around their defenders until he was within shooting distance. He aimed the ball low into the left-hand corner of the net.

GOAL!

Two minutes later the whistle blew. "Well done!" said Mrs Barker as they came off the pitch. "That final goal saved us from defeat – and right at the last minute!"

This time Tod was certain he saw Napoleon on the touchline, standing just behind Mum and Lucy. He gave him the thumbs-up and Napoleon waved back. So did Mum, who must have thought he was looking at her. Tod grinned at her triumphantly and when he looked again, Napoleon had disappeared.

After the match came the tea. Both teams sat at long trestle tables and tucked into sausage rolls, cakes and crisps, washed down with gallons of coke. Tod looked across at Jo Marshall and said, "You played well."

"So did you." She smiled at him. "Is it true you're football-mad and never think about anything else?"

Tod flushed. "Who told you that?"

"Alice. She got it from her cousin."

"It's true I love football," he admitted. "But I'm interested in other things as well. Like history. I know a lot about Napoleon."

"We did a project once about Napoleon," said Jo. "Did you know he fought a battle at Waterloo? That's the same name as our school."

"Yes, I did know that," said Tod with an inward smile.

"He lost it, though. In the end, they put him in prison on an island for the rest of his life. Poor old Napoleon." Jo looked sad. "They say he never got over losing the Battle of Waterloo."

But this time, Tod thought, the battle had not been lost. They hadn't exactly won it – but they hadn't been defeated, either. Surely that must have pleased Napoleon? Somehow he had the feeling he wouldn't be seeing the famous general again.

With a grin he raised his glass of coke. "That was a great match, Jo."

She smiled back at him. "Best ever."

Thanks to Napoleon, Tod added silently.

About the author

I always knew I wanted to be a writer, but I started my working life as a BBC secretary and then became a teacher. My first children's book (about a dinosaur) was written for the dinosaur-mad children in my class and I enjoyed writing it so much that I decided to live dangerously by becoming a full-time writer. Since then I have written over forty books for children of all ages. Best of all, I like writing mysteries and stories that make people laugh.

The idea for this particular story came when I heard a TV football commentator talking about strategy. For some strange reason, this made me think of Napoleon...